How to Plan for Workplace Emergencies and Evacuations

U.S. Department of Labor
Occupational Safety and Health Administration

OSHA 3088
2001 (Revised)

How to Plan for Workplace Emergencies and Evacuations

U.S. Department of Labor
Elaine L. Chao, Secretary

John L. Henshaw, Assistant Secretary
Occupational Safety and Health Administration

OSHA 3088
2001 (Revised)

Contents   Page

Introduction

Nobody expects an emergency or disaster — especially one that affects them, their employees, and their business personally. Yet the simple truth is that emergencies and disasters can strike anyone, anytime, and anywhere. You and your employees could be forced to evacuate your company when you least expect it.

This booklet is designed to help you, the employer, plan for that possibility. The best way to protect yourself, your workers, and your business is to expect the unexpected and develop a well-thought-out emergency action plan to guide you when immediate action is necessary.

What is a workplace emergency?

A workplace emergency is an unforeseen situation that threatens your employees, customers, or the public; disrupts or shuts down your operations; or causes physical or environmental damage. Emergencies may be natural or manmade and include the following:

- Floods,
- Hurricanes,
- Tornadoes,
- Fires,
- Toxic gas releases,
- Chemical spills,
- Radiological accidents,
- Explosions,
- Civil disturbances, and
- Workplace violence resulting in bodily harm and trauma.

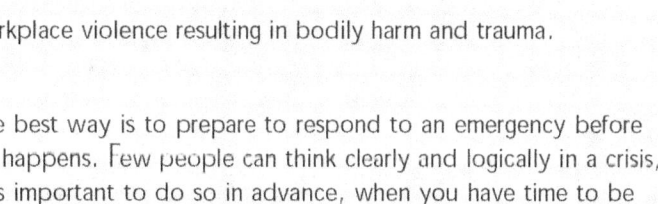

How do you protect yourself, your employees, and your business?

The best way is to prepare to respond to an emergency before it happens. Few people can think clearly and logically in a crisis, so it is important to do so in advance, when you have time to be thorough.

Brainstorm the worst-case scenarios. Ask yourself what you would do if the worst happened. What if a fire broke out in your boiler room? Or a hurricane hit your building head-on? Or a train carrying hazardous waste derailed while passing your loading dock? Once you have identified potential emergencies, consider how they would affect you and your workers and how you would respond.

What is an emergency action plan?

An emergency action plan covers designated actions employers and employees must take to ensure employee safety from fire and other emergencies. Not all employers are required to establish an emergency action plan. See the flowchart on page 11 to determine if you are. Even if you are not specifically required to do so, compiling an emergency action plan is a good way to protect yourself, your employees, and your business during an emergency.

Putting together a comprehensive emergency action plan that deals with all types of issues specific to your worksite is not difficult.

What should your emergency action plan include?

You may find it beneficial to include your management team and employees in the process. Explain your goal of protecting lives and property in the event of an emergency, and ask for their help in establishing and implementing your emergency action plan. Their commitment and support are critical to the plan's success.

When developing your emergency action plan, it's a good idea to look at a wide variety of potential emergencies that could occur in your workplace. It should be tailored to your worksite and include information about all potential sources of emergencies. Developing an emergency action plan means you should do a hazard assessment to determine what, if any, physical or chemical hazards in your workplaces could cause an emergency. If you have more than one worksite, each site should have an emergency action plan.

At a minimum, your emergency action plan must include the following:

- A preferred method for reporting fires and other emergencies;
- An evacuation policy and procedure;
- Emergency escape procedures and route assignments, such as floor plans, workplace maps, and safe or refuge areas;

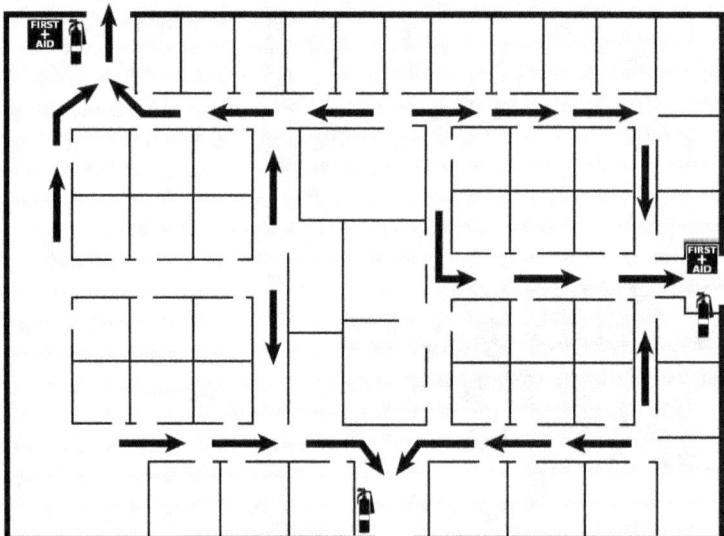

- Names, titles, departments, and telephone numbers of individuals both within and outside your company to contact for additional information or explanation of duties and responsibilities under the emergency plan;
- Procedures for employees who remain to perform or shut down critical plant operations, operate fire extinguishers, or perform other essential services that cannot be shut down for every emergency alarm before evacuating; and
- Rescue and medical duties for any workers designated to perform them.

You also may want to consider designating an assembly location and procedures to account for all employees after an evacuation.

In addition, although they are not specifically required by OSHA, you may find it helpful to include in your plan the following:

- The site of an alternative communications center to be used in the event of a fire or explosion; and

- A secure on- or offsite location to store originals or duplicate copies of accounting records, legal documents, your employees' emergency contact lists, and other essential records.

How do you alert employees to an emergency?

Your plan must include a way to alert employees, including disabled workers, to evacuate or take other action, and how to report emergencies, as required. Among the steps you must take are the following:

- Make sure alarms are distinctive and recognized by all employees as a signal to evacuate the work area or perform actions identified in your plan;

- Make available an emergency communications system such as a public address system, portable radio unit, or other means to notify employees of the emergency and to contact local law enforcement, the fire department, and others; and

- Stipulate that alarms must be able to be heard, seen, or otherwise perceived by everyone in the workplace. You might want to consider providing an auxiliary power supply in the event that electricity is shut off. (*29 CFR* 1910.165(b)(2) offers more information on alarms.)

Although it is not specifically required by OSHA, you also may want to consider the following:

- Using tactile devices to alert employees who would not otherwise be able to recognize an audible or visual alarm; and

- Providing an updated list of key personnel such as the plant manager or physician, in order of priority, to notify in the event of an emergency during off-duty hours.

How do you develop an evacuation policy and procedures?

A disorganized evacuation can result in confusion, injury, and property damage. That is why when developing your emergency action plan it is important to determine the following:

- Conditions under which an evacuation would be necessary;

- A clear chain of command and designation of the person in your business authorized to order an evacuation or shutdown. You may want to designate an "evacuation warden" to assist others in an evacuation and to account for personnel;

- Specific evacuation procedures, including routes and exits. Post these procedures where they are easily accessible to all employees;

- Procedures for assisting people with disabilities or who do not speak English;

- Designation of what, if any, employees will continue or shut down critical operations during an evacuation. These people must be

3

Under what conditions should you call for an evacuation?

capable of recognizing when to abandon the operation and evacuate themselves; and

- A system for accounting for personnel following an evacuation. Consider employees' transportation needs for community-wide evacuations.

In the event of an emergency, local emergency officials may order you to evacuate your premises. In some cases, they may instruct you to shut off the water, gas, and electricity. If you have access to radio or television, listen to newscasts to keep informed and follow whatever official orders you receive.

In other cases, a designated person within your business should be responsible for making the decision to evacuate or shut down operations. Protecting the health and safety of everyone in the facility should be the first priority. In the event of a fire, an immediate evacuation to a predetermined area away from the facility is the best way to protect employees. On the other hand, evacuating employees may not be the best response to an emergency such as a toxic gas release at a facility across town from your business.

The type of building you work in may be a factor in your decision. Most buildings are vulnerable to the effects of disasters such as tornadoes, earthquakes, floods, or explosions. The extent of the damage depends on the type of emergency and the building's construction. Modern factories and office buildings, for example, are framed in steel and are structurally more sound than neighborhood business premises may be. In a disaster such as a major earthquake or explosion, however, nearly every type of structure will be affected. Some buildings will collapse and others will be left with weakened floors and walls.

What is the role of coordinators and evacuation wardens during an emergency?

When drafting your emergency action plan, you may wish to select a responsible individual to lead and coordinate your emergency plan and evacuation. It is critical that employees know who the coordinator is and understand that person has the authority to make decisions during emergencies.

The coordinator should be responsible for the following:

- Assessing the situation to determine whether an emergency exists requiring activation of your emergency procedures;
- Supervising all efforts in the area, including evacuating personnel;

- Coordinating outside emergency services, such as medical aid and local fire departments, and ensuring that they are available and notified when necessary; and
- Directing the shutdown of plant operations when required.

You also may find it beneficial to coordinate the action plan with other employers when several employers share the worksite, although OSHA standards do not specifically require this.

In addition to a coordinator, you may want to designate evacuation wardens to help move employees from danger to safe areas during an emergency. Generally, one warden for every 20 employees should be adequate, and the appropriate number of wardens should be available at all times during working hours.

Employees designated to assist in emergency evacuation procedures should be trained in the complete workplace layout and various alternative escape routes. All employees and those designated to assist in emergencies should be made aware of employees with special needs who may require extra assistance, how to use the buddy system, and hazardous areas to avoid during an emergency evacuation.

How do you establish evacuation routes and exits?

When preparing your emergency action plan, designate primary and secondary evacuation routes and exits. To the extent possible under the conditions, ensure that evacuation routes and emergency exits meet the following conditions:

- Clearly marked and well lit;
- Wide enough to accommodate the number of evacuating personnel;
- Unobstructed and clear of debris at all times; and
- Unlikely to expose evacuating personnel to additional hazards.

If you prepare drawings that show evacuation routes and exits, post them prominently for all employees to see.

How do you account for employees after an evacuation?

Accounting for all employees following an evacuation is critical. Confusion in the assembly areas can lead to delays in rescuing anyone trapped in the building, or unnecessary and dangerous search-and-rescue operations. To ensure the fastest, most accurate accountability of your employees, you may want to consider including these steps in your emergency action plan:

- Designate assembly areas where employees should gather after evacuating;
- Take a head count after the evacuation. Identify the names and last known locations of anyone not accounted for and pass them to the official in charge;
- Establish a method for accounting for non-employees such as suppliers and customers; and

How should you plan for rescue operations?

What medical assistance should you provide during an emergency?

What role should employees play in your emergency action plan?

- Establish procedures for further evacuation in case the incident expands. This may consist of sending employees home by normal means or providing them with transportation to an offsite location.

It takes more than just willing hands to save lives. Untrained individuals may endanger themselves and those they are trying to rescue. For this reason, it is generally wise to leave rescue work to those who are trained, equipped, and certified to conduct rescues.

If you have operations that take place in permit-required confined spaces, you may want your emergency action plan to include rescue procedures that specifically address entry into each confined space. (See also OSHA Publication 3138, *Permit-Required Confined Spaces*, and the National Institute for Occupational Safety and Health (NIOSH) Publication 80-106, *Criteria for a Recommended Standard...Working in Confined Spaces*.)

If your company does not have a formal medical program, you may want to investigate ways to provide medical and first-aid services. If medical facilities are available near your worksite, you can make arrangements for them to handle emergency cases. Provide your employees with a written emergency medical procedure to minimize confusion during an emergency.

If an infirmary, clinic, or hospital is not close to your workplace, ensure that onsite person(s) have adequate training in first aid. The American Red Cross, some insurance providers, local safety councils, fire departments, or other resources may be able to provide this training. Treatment of a serious injury should begin within 3 to 4 minutes of the accident.

Consult with a physician to order appropriate first-aid supplies for emergencies. Medical personnel must be accessible to provide advice and consultation in resolving health problems that occur in the workplace. Establish a relationship with a local ambulance service so transportation is readily available for emergencies.

The best emergency action plans include employees in the planning process, specify what employees should do during an emergency, and ensure that employees receive proper training for emergencies. When you include your employees in your planning, encourage them to offer suggestions about potential hazards, worst-case scenarios, and proper emergency responses. After you develop the plan, review it with your employees to make sure everyone knows what to do before, during and after an emergency.

Keep a copy of your emergency action plan in a convenient location where employees can get to it, or provide all employees a copy. If you have 10 or fewer employees, you may communicate your plan orally.

What employee information should your plan include?

What type of training do your employees need?

In the event of an emergency, it could be important to have ready access to important personal information about your employees. This includes their home telephone numbers, the names and telephone numbers of their next of kin, and medical information.

Educate your employees about the types of emergencies that may occur and train them in the proper course of action. The size of your workplace and workforce, processes used, materials handled, and the availability of onsite or outside resources will determine your training requirements. Be sure all your employees understand the function and elements of your emergency action plan, including types of potential emergencies, reporting procedures, alarm systems, evacuation plans, and shutdown procedures. Discuss any special hazards you may have onsite such as flammable materials, toxic chemicals, radioactive sources, or water-reactive substances. Clearly communicate to your employees who will be in charge during an emergency to minimize confusion.

General training for your employees should address the following:

- Individual roles and responsibilities;
- Threats, hazards, and protective actions;
- Notification, warning, and communications procedures;
- Means for locating family members in an emergency;
- Emergency response procedures;
- Evacuation, shelter, and accountability procedures;
- Location and use of common emergency equipment; and
- Emergency shutdown procedures.

You also may wish to train your employees in first-aid procedures, including protection against bloodborne pathogens; respiratory protection, including use of an escape-only respirator; and methods for preventing unauthorized access to the site.

Once you have reviewed your emergency action plan with your employees and everyone has had the proper training, it is a good idea to hold practice drills as often as necessary to keep employees prepared. Include outside resources such as fire and police departments when possible. After each drill, gather management and employees to evaluate the effectiveness of the drill. Identify the strengths and weaknesses of your plan and work to improve it.

How often do you need to train your employees?

What does your plan need to include about hazardous substances?

Review your plan with all your employees and consider requiring annual training in the plan. Also offer training when you do the following:

- Develop your initial plan;
- Hire new employees;
- Introduce new equipment, materials, or processes into the workplace that affect evacuation routes;
- Change the layout or design of the facility; and
- Revise or update your emergency procedures.

No matter what kind of business you run, you could potentially face an emergency involving hazardous materials such as flammable, explosive, toxic, noxious, corrosive, biological, oxidizable, or radioactive substances.

The source of the hazardous substances could be external, such as a local chemical plant that catches on fire or an oil truck that overturns on a nearby freeway. The source may be within your physical plant. Regardless of the source, these events could have a direct impact on

your employees and your business and should be addressed by your emergency action plan.

If you use or store hazardous substances at your worksite, you face an increased risk of an emergency involving hazardous materials and should

address this possibility in your emergency action plan. OSHA's Hazard Communication Standard (*29 CFR* 1910.1200) requires employers who use hazardous chemicals to inventory them, keep the manufacturer-supplied Material Safety Data Sheets (MSDSs) for them in a place accessible to workers, label containers of these chemicals with their hazards, and train employees in ways to protect themselves against those hazards. A good way to start is to determine from your hazardous chemical inventory what hazardous chemicals you use and to gather the MSDSs for the chemicals. MSDSs describe the hazards that a chemical may present, list the precautions to take when handling, storing, or using the substance, and outline emergency and first-aid procedures.

For specific information on how to respond to emergencies involving hazardous materials and hazardous waste operations, refer to *29 CFR,* Part 1910.120(q) and OSHA Publication 3114, *Hazardous Waste and Emergency Response Operations.* Both are available online at www.osha.gov.

What special equipment should you provide for emergencies?

Your employees may need personal protective equipment to evacuate during an emergency. Personal protective equipment must be based on the potential hazards in the workplace. Assess your workplace to determine potential hazards and the appropriate controls and protective equipment for those hazards. Personal protective equipment may include items such as the following:

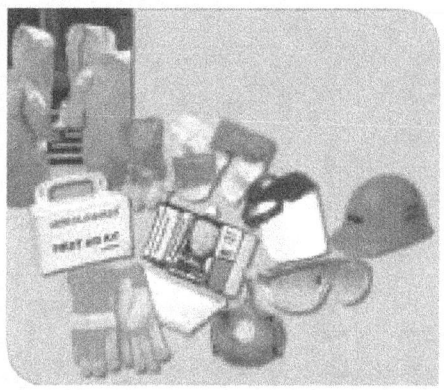

- Safety glasses, goggles, or face shields for eye protection;
- Hard hats and safety shoes for head and foot protection;
- Proper respirators;
- Chemical suits, gloves, hoods, and boots for body protection from chemicals;
- Special body protection for abnormal environmental conditions such as extreme temperatures; and
- Any other special equipment or warning devices necessary for hazards unique to your worksite.

How do you choose appropriate respirators and other equipment?

Consult with health and safety professionals before making any purchases. Respirators selected should be appropriate to the hazards in your workplace, meet OSHA standards criteria, and be certified by the National Institute for Occupational Safety and Health.

Respiratory protection may be necessary if your employees must pass through toxic atmospheres of dust, mists, gases, or vapors, or through oxygen-deficient areas while evacuating. There are four basic categories of respirators for use in different conditions. All respirators must be NIOSH-certified under the current *29 CFR 1910.134*. See also OSHA's *Small Entity Compliance Guide for Respiratory Protection, 1999*, online at www.osha.gov.

Who should you coordinate with when drafting your emergency action plan?

Although there is no specific OSHA requirement to do so, you may find it useful to coordinate your efforts with any other companies or employee groups in your building to ensure the effectiveness of your plan. In addition, if you rely on assistance from local emergency responders such as the fire department, local HAZMAT teams, or other outside responders, you may find it useful to coordinate your emergency plans with these organizations. This ensures that you are aware of the capabilities of these outside responders and that they know what you expect of them.

What are OSHA's requirements for emergencies?

Some of the key OSHA requirements for emergencies can be found in the following sections of the agency's General Industry Occupational Safety and Health Standards (*29 CFR* 1910).

Subpart E – Means of Egress

1910.37	Means of egress
1910.38	Employee emergency plans and fire prevention plans
Appendix	Means of egress

Subpart H – Hazardous Materials

1910.119	Process safety management of highly hazardous chemicals
1910.120	Hazardous waste operations and emergency response

Subpart I – Personal Protective Equipment

1910.133	Eye and face protection
1910.134	Respiratory protection
1910.135	Occupational head protection
1910.136	Occupational foot protection
1910.138	Hand protection

Subpart J – General Environmental Controls

1910.146	Permit-required confined spaces
1910.147	Control of hazardous energy sources

Subpart K – Medical and First Aid

1910.151	Medical services and first aid

Subpart L – Fire Protection

1910.155-156	Fire protection and fire brigades
1910.157-163	Fire suppression equipment
1910.164	Fire detection systems
1910.165	Employee alarm systems
Appendices A-E of Subpart L	

Subpart R – Special Industries, Electrical Power Generation, Transmission, and Distribution

Subpart Z – Toxic and Hazardous Substances

1910.1030	Bloodborne pathogens
1910.1200	Hazard communication

What other OSHA standards address emergency planning requirements?

In addition to *29 CFR* 1910.38(a), several other OSHA standards address emergency planning requirements. These include the *29 CFR* 1910.120(q), *Hazardous Waste Operations and Emergency Response*; *29 CFR* 1910.156, *Fire Brigades*; and *29 CFR* 1910.146(k), *Permit-Required Confined Spaces*. The OSHA Publication 3122, *Principal Emergency Response and Preparedness Requirements in OSHA Standards and Guidance for Safety and Health Problems*, provides a broad view of emergency planning requirements across OSHA standards.

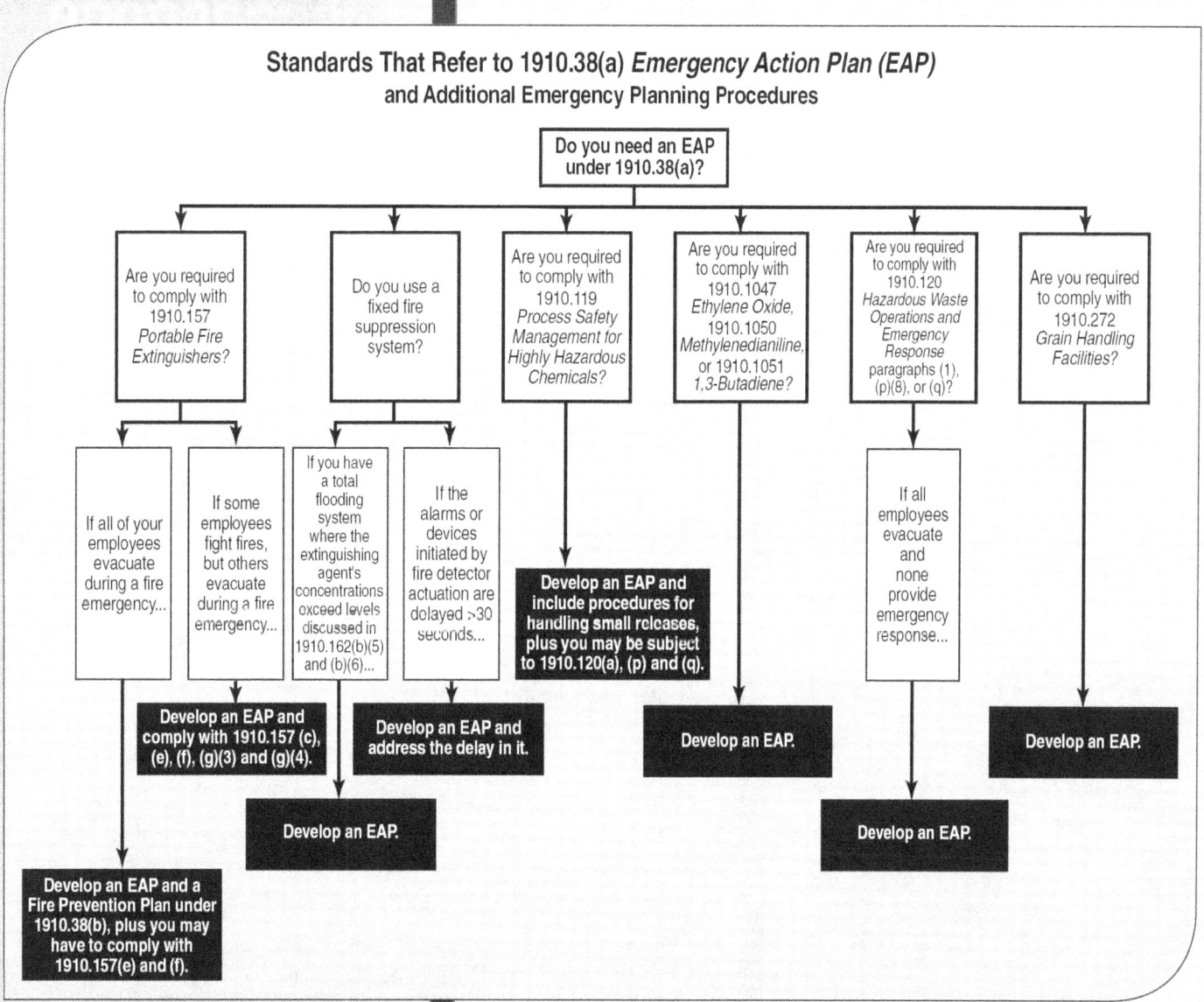

Standards That Refer to 1910.38(a) *Emergency Action Plan (EAP)* and Additional Emergency Planning Procedures

Do you need an EAP under 1910.38(a)?

- Are you required to comply with 1910.157 *Portable Fire Extinguishers?*
  - If all of your employees evacuate during a fire emergency...
    - **Develop an EAP and a Fire Prevention Plan under 1910.38(b), plus you may have to comply with 1910.157(e) and (f).**
  - If some employees fight fires, but others evacuate during a fire emergency...
    - **Develop an EAP and comply with 1910.157 (c), (e), (f), (g)(3) and (g)(4).**

- Do you use a fixed fire suppression system?
  - If you have a total flooding system where the extinguishing agent's concentrations exceed levels discussed in 1910.162(b)(5) and (b)(6)...
    - **Develop an EAP.**
  - If the alarms or devices initiated by fire detector actuation are delayed >30 seconds...
    - **Develop an EAP and address the delay in it.**

- Are you required to comply with 1910.119 *Process Safety Management for Highly Hazardous Chemicals?*
  - **Develop an EAP and include procedures for handling small releases, plus you may be subject to 1910.120(a), (p) and (q).**

- Are you required to comply with 1910.1047 *Ethylene Oxide*, 1910.1050 *Methylenedianiline*, or 1910.1051 *1,3-Butadiene?*
  - **Develop an EAP.**

- Are you required to comply with 1910.120 *Hazardous Waste Operations and Emergency Response* paragraphs (1), (p)(8), or (q)?
  - If all employees evacuate and none provide emergency response...
    - **Develop an EAP.**

- Are you required to comply with 1910.272 *Grain Handling Facilities?*
  - **Develop an EAP.**

What assistance does OSHA provide?

OSHA provides a wide range of references and services to help employers and employees improve workplace health and safety and comply with regulatory requirements. These include the following:

- Education and training opportunities,
- Publications,
- Electronic services,
- Free onsite consultation services, and
- Participation in the Voluntary Protection Programs.

To file a complaint, report an emergency, or seek OSHA advice, assistance, or products, call 1-800-321 OSHA or your nearest regional office, listed in Appendix 1. The teletypewriter (TTY) number is 1-877-889-5627.

Information on these and other OSHA programs and services is posted on the agency website at www.osha.gov.

What education and training does OSHA offer?

OSHA area offices offer a variety of information services including publications, audiovisual aids, technical advice, and speakers for special engagements.

In addition, OSHA's Training Institute in Des Plaines, IL, provides basic and advanced courses in safety and health for federal and state compliance officers, state consultants, federal agency employees, and private-sector employers, employees, and their representatives.

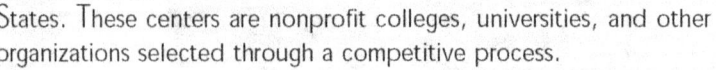

Due to the high demand for OSHA Training Institute courses, OSHA Training Institute Education Centers also offer them at sites throughout the United States. These centers are nonprofit colleges, universities, and other organizations selected through a competitive process.

OSHA also provides grants to nonprofit organizations to conduct specialized workplace training and education not available from other sources. Grants are awarded annually. Recipients contribute 20 percent of the total grant cost.

For more information on grants, training, and education, contact the OSHA Training Institute, Office of Training and Education by mail at 1555 Times Drive, Des Plaines IL 60018; by phone at (847) 297-4810, or by fax at (847) 297-4874.

What other publications does OSHA offer?

OSHA offers more than 100 documents, including brochures, fact sheets, posters, pocket cards, flyers, technical documents, and a quarterly magazine. These documents are available online at www.osha.gov or by calling (202) 693-1888. Among the titles are the following:

- *Access to Medical and Exposure Records* – OSHA 3110
- *All About OSHA* – OSHA 2056
- *Chemical Hazard Communication* – OSHA 3084
- *Consultation Services for the Employer* – OSHA 3047
- *Controlling Electrical Hazards* – OSHA 3075
- *Employer Rights and Responsibilities Following an OSHA Inspection* – OSHA 3000
- *Employee Workplace Rights* – OSHA 3021
- *Hazardous Waste and Emergency Response* – OSHA 3114
- *Job Hazard Analysis* – OSHA 3071
- *OSHA Handbook for Small Business* – OSHA 2209
- *Personal Protective Equipment* – OSHA 3077
- *Respirator Protection* – OSHA 3079

What electronic services does OSHA provide?

OSHA standards, interpretations, directives, and additional information are posted on the agency's website at www.osha.gov. Visits to the site continue to increase, with nearly 1.4 million visitors using the site each month for a total of 23 million hits.

Among the popular Internet offerings are electronic tools to help small businesses understand and comply with OSHA regulations and promote safety and health in their workplaces. These e-Tools include the Expert Advisors, interactive software programs that help businesses identify workplace hazards. By answering a few simple questions on their computer screens, employers get reliable answers on how OSHA regulations apply to their unique work sites.

Another popular Internet product is eCATS, OSHA's electronic Compliance Assistance Tools, which help businesses identify and correct workplace hazards. A totally new generation of e-Tools coming soon will combine both decision tree logic software and graphics, giving users enhanced capabilities and the best of both worlds.

In addition, a wide variety of OSHA materials including standards, interpretations, directives, and more can be purchased on CD-ROM from the Government Printing Office. To order, write to Superintendent of Documents, U.S. Government Printing Office, Washington, DC 20402. Specify *OSHA Regulations, Documents and Technical Information on CD-ROM, (ORDT)*, S/N 729-1300000-5. The price is $45 per year ($57.50 overseas); single copy $17 ($21.25 overseas).

What free onsite consultation services does OSHA provide?

The OSHA Consultation Service offers free onsite safety and health consultation services to help employers establish and maintain safe and healthful workplaces. The service is funded largely by OSHA and is delivered by professional safety and health consultants within state governments. Developed primarily for smaller employers with more hazardous operations, the service includes an appraisal of all mechanical systems, physical work practices, environmental workplace hazards, and all aspects of the employer's job safety and health program.

The onsite consultation program is separate from OSHA's inspection efforts. No penalties are proposed or citations issued for safety or health problems identified by an OSHA consultant. The service is confidential. The employer's and firm's name, and any information about the workplace, including any unsafe or unhealthful working conditions the consultant identifies, are not reported routinely to the OSHA inspection staff. The employer, however, is obligated to correct any serious job safety and health hazards identified in a timely manner, and commits to do so when requesting the service.

For more information, see Appendix 3 for a list of contact telephone numbers.

What are the Voluntary Protection Programs?

The Voluntary Protection Programs, or VPPs, recognize and promote effective safety and health program management. Companies in the VPP have strong safety and health programs, implemented and managed cooperatively by their management and labor forces in cooperation with OSHA. Sites approved for VPP's three programs – Star, Merit, and Demonstration – meet and maintain rigorous standards. Benefits to participants include the following:

- Lost-workday case rates generally 60 to 80 percent below industry averages;
- Reduced workers' compensation and other injury- and illness-related costs;
- Improved employee motivation to work safely, leading to better quality and productivity;
- Positive community recognition and interaction;
- Further improvement and revitalization of already good safety and health programs; and
- Partnership with OSHA.

For more information, contact the VPP manager in your OSHA regional office, visit OSHA's website, or see Appendix 1 for a list of telephone numbers.

What partnership opportunities does OSHA provide?

OSHA has initiated partnerships with employers, employees, and employee representatives in a wide range of industries to encourage, assist, and recognize efforts to eliminate workplace hazards. Participants work together to identify a common goal, develop plans to achieve it, and implement those plans in a cooperative way. Partnerships can transform relationships between OSHA and an employer or entire industry. Former adversaries recognize that working together to solve workplace safety and health problems is to everyone's advantage.

For more information, contact your OSHA regional office. See Appendix 1 for a list of telephone numbers.

What is the value of a good safety and health program?

A good, effectively managed worker safety and health program can be a big factor in reducing work-related injuries and illnesses and their related costs. OSHA offers voluntary guidelines to help employers and employees in workplaces it covers develop effective safety and health programs. *Safety and Health Program Management Guidelines (Federal Register* 54(18): 3908-3916, January 26, 1989) identifies four general elements critical to a successful safety and health management program. These are:

- Management leadership and employee involvement;
- An analysis of worksite hazards;
- Use of hazard prevention and control initiatives; and
- Safety and health training.

These guidelines are posted on the OSHA website at www.osha-slc.gov/FedReg_osha_data/FED19890126.html. See also OSHA's Safety and Health Management Systems eCAT at www.osha-slc.gov/SLTC/safetyhealthecat/index.html.

What is the role of state programs?

The *Occupational Safety and Health Act of 1970* encourages states to develop and operate their own job safety and health plans. States that do so must adopt standards and enforce requirements that are at least as effective as federal requirements. Twenty-four states and two territories have adopted their own plans, three of which cover only public employees. For more information, visit OSHA's website and see Appendix 2 for a listing of states and territories with approved plans.

What other groups or associations can help me?

Various organizations can provide you with safety and health information that may help you in formulating your emergency action plan. A few are listed here.

Safety Data Sheets, Guides and Manuals

- *AIHA Hygienic Guide Series.* American Industrial Hygiene Association, 2700 Prosperity Avenue, Fairfax, VA 22031.
- *ANSI Standards, Z37 Series, Acceptable Concentrations of Toxic Dusts and Gases.* American National Standards Institute, 11 West 42nd Street, New York, NY 10036.

- *ASTM Standards and Related Material.* American Society for Testing and Materials, 1916 Race Street, Philadelphia, PA 19103.

Safety Standards and Specifications Groups

- American National Standards Institute, 11 West 42nd Street, New York, NY 10036. Coordinates and administers the federal voluntary standardization system in the United States.

- American Society for Testing and Materials, 1916 Race Street, Philadelphia, PA 19103. The world's largest source of voluntary consensus standards for materials, products, systems, and services.

Fire Protection Organizations

- Factory Insurance Association, 85 Woodland Street, Hartford, CT 06105. Composed of capital stock insurance companies that provide engineering, inspection, and loss-adjustment services.

- Factory Mutual System, 1151 Boston-Providence Turnpike, Norwood, MA 02062. An industrial fire protection, engineering, and inspection bureau established by mutual fire insurance companies.

- National Fire Protection Association, 470 Batterymarch Park, Quincy, MA 02269. A clearinghouse for information on fire protection and prevention as well as NFPA standards.

- Underwriter Laboratories, Inc., 207 East Ohio Street, Chicago, IL 60611. A nonprofit organization that publishes annual lists of manufacturers that provide products meeting appropriate standards.

Appendices

OSHA Regional Offices

REGION I
(CT,* ME, MA, NH, RI, VT*)
JFK Federal Building, Room E340
Boston, MA 02203
(617) 565-9860

REGION II
(NJ,* PR,* VI*)
201 Varick Street, Room 670
New York, NY 10014
(212) 337-2378

REGION III
(DE, DC, MD,* PA,* VA,* WV)
The Curtis Center
170 S. Independence Mall West
Suite 740 West
Philadelphia, PA 19106-3309
(215) 861-4900

REGION IV
(AL, FL, GA, KY,* MS, NC,* SC,* TN*)
Atlanta Federal Center
61 Forsyth Street, SW, Room 6T50
Atlanta, GA 30303
(404) 562-2300

REGION V
(IL, IN,* MI,* MN,* OH, WI)
230 South Dearborn Street, Room 3244
Chicago, IL 60604
(312) 353-2220

REGION VI
(AR, LA, NM,* OK, TX)
525 Griffin Street, Room 602
Dallas, TX 75202
(214) 767-4731 or 4736 x224

REGION VII
(IA,* KS, MO, NE)
City Center Square
1100 Main Street, Suite 800
Kansas City, MO 64105
(816) 426-5861

REGION VIII
(CO, MT, ND, SD, UT,* WY*)
1999 Broadway, Suite 1690
Denver, CO 80202-5716
(303) 844-1600

REGION IX
(American Samoa, AZ,* CA,* HI, NV*)
71 Stevenson Street, Room 420
San Francisco, CA 94105
(415) 975-4310

REGION X
(AK,* ID, OR,* WA*)
1111 Third Avenue, Suite 715
Seattle, WA 98101-3212
(206) 553-5930

* These states and territories operate their own OSHA-approved job safety and health programs (Connecticut, New Jersey, and New York plans cover public employees only). States with approved programs must have a standard that is identical to, or at least as effective as, the federal standard.

OSHA Area Offices

Birmingham, AL	(205) 731-1534
Mobile, AL	(334) 441-6131
Anchorage, AK	(907) 271-5152
Phoenix, AZ	(602) 640-2348
Little Rock, AR	(501) 324-6291(5818)
San Diego, CA	(619) 557-5909
Sacramento, CA	(916) 566-7471
Denver, CO	(303) 844-5285
Englewood, CO	(303) 843-4500
Bridgeport, CT	(203) 579-5581
Hartford, CT	(860) 240-3152
Wilmington, DE	(302) 573-6518
Fort Lauderdale, FL	(954) 424-0242
Jacksonville, FL	(904) 232-2895
Tampa, FL	(813) 626-1177
Savannah, GA	(912) 652-4393
Smyrna, GA	(770) 984-8700
Tucker, GA	(770) 493-6644/6742
Boise, ID	(208) 321-2960
Calumet City, IL	(708) 891-3800
Des Plaines, IL	(847) 803-4800
Fairview Heights, IL	(618) 632-8612
North Aurora, IL	(630) 896-8700
Peoria, IL	(309) 671-7033
Indianapolis, IN	(317) 226-7290
Des Moines, IA	(515) 284-4794
Wichita, KS	(316) 269-6644
Frankfort, KY	(502) 227-7024
Baton Rouge, LA	(225) 389-0474/0431
Bangor, ME	(207) 941-8177
Portland, ME	(207) 780-3178
August, ME	(207) 622-8417
Linthicum, MD	(410) 865-2055/2056

Braintree, MA .... (617) 565-6924
Methuen, MA .... (617) 565-8110
Springfield, MA .... (413) 785-0123
Lansing, MI .... (517) 327-0904
Minneapolis, MN .... (612) 664-5460

Jackson, MS .... (601) 965-4606
Kansas City, MO .... (816) 483-9531
St. Louis, MO .... (314) 425-4289
Billings, MT .... (406) 247-7494
Raleigh, NC .... (919) 856-4770

Omaha, NE .... (402) 221-3182
Carson City, NV .... (775) 885-6963
Concord, NH .... (603) 225-1629
Avenel, NJ .... (732) 750-3270
Hasbrouck Heights, NJ .... (201) 288-1700

Marlton, NJ .... (609) 757-5181
Parsippany, NJ .... (973) 263-1003
Albuquerque, NM .... (505) 248-5302
Albany, NY .... (518) 464-4338
Bayside, NY .... (718) 279-9060

Bowmansville, NY .... (716) 684-3891
North Syracuse, NY .... (315) 451-0808
Tarrytown, NY .... (914) 524-7510
Westbury, NY .... (516) 334-3344
Bismark, ND .... (701) 250-4521

Cincinnati, OH .... (513) 841-4132
Cleveland, OH .... (216) 522-3818
Columbus, OH .... (614) 469-5582
Toledo, OH .... (419) 259-7542
Oklahoma City, OK .... (405) 231-5351/5389

Portland, OR .... (503) 326-2251
Allentown, PA .... (610) 776-0592
Erie, PA .... (814) 833-5758
Harrisburg, PA .... (717) 782-3902
Philadelphia, PA .... (215) 597-4955

Pittsburgh, PA .... (412) 395-4903
Wilkes-Barre, PA .... (570) 826-6538
Guaynabo, PR .... (787) 277-1560
Providence, RI .... (401) 528-4669
Columbia, SC .... (803) 765-5904

Nashville, TN .... (615) 781-5423
Austin, TX .... (512) 916-5783/5788
Corpus Christi, TX .... (512) 888-3420
Dallas, TX .... (214) 320-2400/2558
El Paso, TX .... (915) 534-6251

Fort Worth, TX .... (817) 428-2470
                                               (485-7647)
Houston, TX .... (281) 591-2438/2787
Houston, TX .... (281) 286-0583/0584
Lubbock, TX .... (806) 472-7681/7685
Salt Lake City, UT .... (801) 530-6901

Norfolk, VA .... (757) 441-3820
Bellevue, WA .... (206) 553-7520
Charleston, WV .... (304) 347-5937
Appleton, WI .... (920) 734-4521
Eau Claire, WI .... (715) 832-9019

Madison, WI .... (608) 264-5388
Milwaukee, WI .... (414) 297-3315

Appendix 2
OSHA-Approved Safety and Health Plans

Juneau, AK .... (907) 465-2700
Phoenix, AZ .... (602) 542-5795
San Francisco, CA .... (415) 703-5050
Wethersfield, CT .... (860) 566-5123
Honolulu, HI .... (808) 586-8844

Indianapolis, ID .... (317) 232-2378
Des Moines, IA .... (515) 281-3447
Indianapolis, IN .... (317) 232-3325
Frankfort, KY .... (502) 564-3070
Baltimore, MD .... (410) 767-2215

Lansing, MI .... (517) 373-7230
St. Paul, MN .... (651) 296-2342
Raleigh, NC .... (919) 807-2900
Trenton, NJ .... (609) 292-2975
Santa Fe, NM .... (505) 827-2850

Carson City, NV .... (775) 687-3032
Albany, NY .... (518) 457-2741
Salem, OR .... (503) 378-3272
Hato Rey, PR .... (787) 754-2119
Columbia, SC .... (803) 896-4300

Nashville, TN .... (615) 741-2582
Salt Lake City, UT .... (801) 530-6901
Richmond, VA .... (804) 786-2377
Christiansted, St. Croix, VI .... (340) 773-1990
Montpelier VT .... (802) 828-2288

Olympia, WA .... (360) 902-4200
                                              (360) 902-5430
Cheyenne, WY .... (307) 777-7786

Appendix 3
OSHA Consultation Offices

Anchorage, AK .... (907) 269-4957
Tuscaloosa, AL .... (205) 348-3033
Little Rock, AR .... (501) 682-4522
Phoenix, AZ .... (602) 542-1695
Sacramento, CA .... (916) 574-2555

Fort Collins, CO .... (970) 491-6151
Wethersfield, CT .... (860) 566-4550
Washington, DC .... (202) 541-3727
Wilmington, DE .... (302) 761-8219

Tampa, FL .... (813) 974-9962
Atlanta, GA .... (404) 894-2643
Tiyam, GU .... 9-1-(671) 475-1101
Honolulu, HI .... (808) 586-9100
Des Moines, IA .... (515) 281-7629

Boise, ID .... (208) 426-3283
Chicago, IL .... (312) 814-2337
Indianapolis, IN .... (317) 232-2688
Topeka, KS .... (785) 296-7476
Frankfort, KY .... (502) 564-6895

Baton Rouge, LA .... (225) 342-9601
West Newton, MA .... (617) 727-3982
Laurel, MD .... (410) 880-4970
Augusta, ME .... (207) 624-6460
Lansing, MI .... (517) 322-1809

Saint Paul, MN .... (651) 297-2393
Jefferson City, MO .... (573) 751-3403
Jackson, MS .... (601) 987-3981
Helena, MT .... (406) 444-6418
Raleigh, NC .... (919) 807-2905

Bismarck, ND .... (701) 328-5188
Lincoln, NE .... (402) 471-4717
Concord, NH .... (603) 271-2024
Trenton, NJ .... (609) 292-3923
Santa Fe, NM .... (505) 827-4230

Albany, NY .... (518) 457-2238
Henderson, NV .... (702) 486-9140
Columbus, OH .... (614) 644-2631
Oklahoma City, OK .... (405) 528-1500
Salem, OR .... (503) 378-3272

Indiana, PA .... (724) 357-2396
Hato Rey, PR .... (787) 754-2171
Providence, RI .... (401) 222-2438
Columbia, SC .... (803) 734-9614
Brookings, SD .... (605) 688-4101

Nashville, TN .... (615) 741-7036
Austin, TX .... (512) 804-4640
Salt Lake City, UT .... (801) 530-6901
Montepilier, VT .... (802) 828-2765
Richmond, VA .... (804) 786-6359

Christiansted St. Croix, VI .... (809) 772-1315
Olympia, WA .... (360) 902-5638
Madison, WI .... (608) 266-9383
Waukesha, WI .... (262) 523-3044
Charleston, WV .... (304) 558-7890
Cheyenne, WY .... (307) 777-7786